Arun's Adventures: A Collection of Children's Poems

Erika Rathi

BookLeaf Publishing

India | USA | UK

Presentation by *BookLeaf Publishing*

Web: www.bookleafpub.com

E-mail: info@bookleafpub.com

ISBN: 9789360941208

First edition 2024

~Bablu & Babli~

By: Rajveer Choudhary

*To Rajveer & Ranveer Choudhary,
and Luca Farina*

*You are the stars that light up my sky, the fuel
that ignites my imagination, and the pillars of
my strength. This book is dedicated to each of
you, whose boundless curiosity, infectious
laughter, and unwavering love have filled my
life with joy and inspiration.*

*Rajveer & Ranveer, your adventurous spirits
and endless desire for exploration remind me of
the wonders of childhood. May you always dare
to dream, discover, and delight in the magic of
the world around you.*

*Luca, your playful antics and infectious giggle
bring warmth to every moment. May you
continue to find joy in the simplest of pleasures,
and never lose sight of the beauty that
surrounds you.*

With love and gratitude,

Erika Farina Rathi

ACKNOWLEDGEMENT

First and foremost, I extend my deepest regards to my dearest husband Aviraj for his unwavering support and belief in my creative endeavours, without you I would not have had the courage to do this.

And to my entire family, both old and new,
thank you for always encouraging me:
(Claudio & Sylvia, Alec & Fanny,
Arvind & Charul, Millie & Prashant)

I am indebted to my mom whose love and guidance has kept my childhood innocence and curiosity alive, thank you for nurturing my imagination and instilling in me a lifelong love of learning - *you're simply the best.*

Lastly, I would like to express my heartfelt gratitude to Sadhana Rao for the time she dedicated and her incredible patience during the editing process. Your guidance and kindness have been invaluable, helping me navigate challenges and realize my vision.

PREFACE

Dear Readers,

It is with immense joy that I present to you this collection of children's poems, "Arun's Adventures." Before we delve into the whimsical world of Arun and his escapades across India, I would like to take a moment to share with you the credibility behind the authorship and the inspiration behind these verses.

With an honors degree in Liberal Arts, I have always been drawn to the power of storytelling as a means of connecting hearts and minds. Through "Arun's Adventures," my intent is not only to entertain but also to educate and inspire young readers.

As the author of this book, I am privileged to be a witness to the enchanting tapestry of India, having moved here several years ago from Canada. My experiences, interactions, and explorations in this captivating and colorful country have inspired the creation of these poems.

But beyond my own experiences, I have also had the privilege of witnessing the magic of storytelling firsthand through the eyes of my nephews. Their innocent stories are a gentle reminder that as we get older…we sometimes forget that there is beauty in everyday life. However, if we know where to look, we can find magic in every situation.

Whether you are a child discovering the wonders
of India for the first time or an adult revisiting
cherished memories, may these poems transport
you to a world of joy, discovery,
and endless possibilities.

TABLE OF CONTENTS

Finding Chikoo

Little Arun was born in New Delhi,
on a sunny day in June.
Into the arms of his loving parents,
Arun arrived when the clock struck noon.

By the time he was five years old,
he already loved to travel and explore.
Arun climbed big trees, rode his bike downhill,
but he still dreamed of something more.

Every night, he sat and prayed,
asking for a companion to have by his side -
someone to accompany him to the park,
and to sit with during long car rides.

The truth is, little Arun
really wanted a dog of his own -
a puppy to love and spend time with,
and to bring into his home.

In his heart, Arun knew that one day
his prayers would surely be met.
But what happened randomly
on a gloomy afternoon,
was something he did not expect.

Arun and his dad were walking home,
while it was drizzling rain outside -
when his dad noticed an animal
under his car, desperately trying to hide.

Arun was distracted by the rain
so at first, he did not see...
stranded right before his eyes
was a tiny, brown puppy!

When Arun peeked under the car,
he and the dog instantly locked eyes.
The dog then crawled out timidly,
and released a woeful cry.

Arun's dad walked towards the dog,
and picked him up from the floor.
Together the two boys ran back home,
and started knocking on the door.

*"Mommy! Mommy! Open up,
we really need your help!"*
After Arun started to weep,
the little dog let out a yelp.

His mom ran to open the door
and to her great surprise:
that along with Arun and his dad,
a sad dog met her eyes.

His paws were covered in thick mud,
and he was shivering from head to toe.
How to help out this frail puppy,
was something that Arun did not know.

His mom quickly grabbed a towel,
and wrapped the dog up nice and tight.
She gave him food, water, and a warm bath,
and tucked him in for the night.

Once the puppy was feeling better,
Arun's mom asked him to come inside.
So that he could see the cute little dog,
with clean fur that had been dried.

The moment Arun stepped into the room,
the dog opened up its eyes.
It got up from the warm cozy bed,
and went to sit by Arun's side.

Arun picked up the dog
and before he could even ask,
his mom said to him with a smile,
"It has finally happened, at last!"

*"We have also been waiting all along
to bring a dog into our home.
But we wanted one to choose you first,
and accept you as its own."*

*"And now that you have a dog,
do you know what you will do?"*
Arun replied:
*"There's only one thing I know for certain:
his name will be Chikoo!"*

A Drive to the Hills

Little Arun was only five years old
when a story of adventure, first was told:
to him, by his mom, of her special place -
with beautiful views and a mountain's embrace.

The place is Mussoorie, way way up high,
in the Himalayan mountains that touch the sky!
"But how will we get there?" Little Arun asked,
"It is so far, it seems like such a hard task!"

His mom gave him a smile,
as she started to say:
"If we leave right now,
we will reach there today!"

Arun asked, *"But how can that be...*
is there a road that high?
I thought you needed
airplanes to touch the sky?"

Arun was in disbelief
when he sat in the car.
As he gazed out the window,
the mountains seemed far.

"We will never reach!"
He continued to say:
*"Not by tomorrow, not in a week,
impossible in a day!"*

His dad started to laugh,
and told him: *"Just wait and see!
Fasten your seatbelt,
and count down from three."*

3, 2, 1 - the car turned on,
the engine let out a loud roar!
Could it be that this car had wings,
and was now ready to soar?

Arun was confused, so he asked again:
*"How will we fly?
By car we absolutely cannot get
to the mountains so high!"*

Arun did not know that
there is a magic road,
that had been built long before,
so this story could be told.

Through this long, winding road,
surrounded by trees,
you can venture to the peak,
from which you can see:
the valleys, so vast,
and the many mountains that rise,
merging together with the big blue skies.

And so, they began their journey to the peak.
Hours went by, *"This will surely take a week!"*
Little Arun said again to his mum,
unaware that half the journey was already done.

Arun fell asleep,
while his dad continued to drive.
Little did Arun know,
that soon they would arrive.

Arun's sleep was suddenly broken
by the sound of Chikoo's bark.
He looked outside, and to his surprise,
it was bright and not yet dark!

Suddenly, his dad parked the car,
and his parents guided him outside.
His mom then asked,
"Arun, did you enjoy the ride?"

Little Arun looked around,
and to his great surprise:
they had reached the mountaintop,
he was now way, way up high!

While being surrounded by fluffy clouds,
Arun felt powerful and tall.
And in that moment he actually forgot,
that he was ever small.

And now he understood,
why this is his mom's favorite place…
standing on top of the world,
within the mountain's embrace.

Aam-mazing Mangoes - Part 1

Arun and his nana
went for a walk,
in the month of June,
when it was hot.

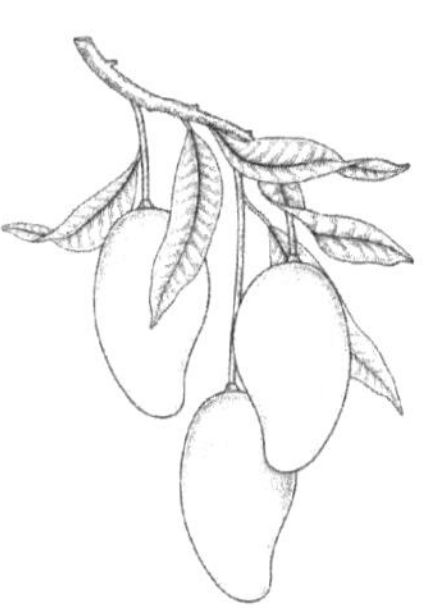

And when he looked up,
little Arun could see:
so many mangoes
hanging from a tree!

*"But where did they come from?
How did they grow?"*
The answers to these questions,
he hoped his nana would know.

Arun's nana smiled and replied:
*"I am glad that you asked...
for many months, in the sun,
this mango tree basked.
And then the mangoes started to grow!
Just know that the process is very slow."*

"I don't remember this tree."
Little Arun questioned:
"Was it always here?"

His nana responded,
*"No, your mom and I had secretly
planted it for you, at this time, last year!"*

Nana continued,
*"But last year it was small,
and it had to get strong.
So it could grow mangoes
all summer long."*

His nana kept on walking,
and they left the tree behind.
While doing rounds of the park,
only one thing was on Arun's mind.

Arun really wanted to taste
the fresh fruit from the tree.
But being still so small,
he couldn't reach any easily.

Desperately, Arun asked his nana
if he could get one down.
To which, his nana replied,
"I'm afraid they're too high from the ground!"

Little Arun, caring for his nana,
didn't want to make him feel bad.
Although, not getting one of the mangoes
left Arun feeling sad.

"That's okay!"
Arun proceeded to say,
*"I am sure there are more
mango trees along the way!"*

But to his dismay…
there were none.
And his walk went from being great,
to not at all fun.

His nana said:
*"Arun, I can see that you're sad.
I'll try to find you some mangoes,
when I go to the market with your dad."*

*"Can we now head back home?
I told your mom we'd be back by three.
And who knows, maybe there'll be a surprise
waiting for you and me."*

Aam-mazing Mangoes - Part 2

Arun and his nana crossed the park,
heading home towards the front door.
Arun was sure that inside his house,
everything was as they had left it before.

But inside sat his mom, patiently waiting,
with a mango in her hand.
Where'd she get the mango from?
He thought to himself.
Arun could not yet understand...

His mom instructed him to go to the kitchen
because in there, nana had kept a surprise.
And that is when he saw
a bucket full of fresh mangoes,
which brought happy tears to his eyes.

There were so many mangoes,
and Arun did not know
which one he should choose...
they all looked so delicious,
how could he pick one
and the others refuse?

His nana came to help,
and taught little Arun the way:
to pick the perfect mango
every time, every day.

"First you look at the color,
and then you look at the size.
You take it in your hands,
and gently squeeze it on both sides."

"If you can easily press it,
then it is ready to eat!
Give it a rinse, my little Arun,
and get ready for your treat!"

Arun sat at the table,
eagerly waiting for someone to assist.
His nana took the mango,
and at the top made a little rip.

Like from the straw of a juice box,
Arun was told to drink the pulpy delight.
Holding the mango with both of his hands,
while making sure to grip it tight.

When he was finished with his mango,
Arun looked up at his nana to see -
if Nana was done with mango number one,
but he was already on mango number three!

They all laughed and smiled,
it ended up being a terrific day.
And little Arun now knew there
were plenty of juicy mangoes,
ready to eat, kept aside on display.

Arun goes to a Buffet

One bite,
Two bites,
Three bites,
Four!
Arun is eating so many
things that he adores.

Five bites,
Six bites,
Seven bites,
Eight!
Arun gets up to make
a second plate.

He has eaten enough,
Arun should really stop.
After nine big bites,
Arun's buttons might pop.

Ten bites down,
and he should now be done.
After eleven bites, he wonders:
"What have I begun?"

Twelve bites in,
and Arun's pants are tight.
After thirteen bites,
there's still no end in sight.

Arun actually thought that
he could make it to fourteen...
But after two whole plates,
his face is turning green.

Arun's tummy is almost bursting,
he's scared he might explode.
He's eaten way too much food,
more than his little stomach can hold.

What if he throws up?
Why didn't he pace?
There are stains on his shirt,
and crumbs on his face.

Arun's now laying on the bench,
he's desperately trying to ignore:
how uncomfortable he's feeling,
he can't take it anymore!

Arun closes his eyes
trying to get some relief.
Before even realizing it,
he drifts off to sleep.

His dad picks Arun up,
and takes him to the car.
He gently sets him in his seat,
thankfully the house is not far.

They reach home,
and his dad carries him to bed.
Arun is dreaming of food:
"Please no more bread!"
Arun cries out in his sleep,
he then opens his eyes.
He is home at last,
what a pleasant surprise!

His mom tucks him in,
and asks if he is okay.
Arun replies, *"I am so painfully full,
I shouldn't have eaten so much today."*

*"But I learned my lesson,
next time I'll pace…
I'll only eat one plate,
because a buffet is not a race."*

Arun's Weekend Getaway - Part 1

Illustration by Rujuta Modia

It was the end of the school year,
and Arun had earned good grades.
His parents decided to reward him,
with a trip to his favorite place.

That magical place is a resort,
by the name of Namaste Dwaar.
Located in the vibrant countryside,
it is only 2 hours away by car!

Arun adores this special place,
for weekends, holidays, and much more.
There's always something fun to do,
and new places for him to explore.

Arun's absolute favourite thing about this resort:
is the big red tractor parked outside.
And as soon as they arrived at the property,
he was ready for his ride.

Arun ran up to the tractor,
and jumped into the carriage in the back.
Then his mom, dad, and Chikoo sat with him,
eagerly waiting to start their ride on the track.

The tractor driver climbed in,
and turned the engine on.
Deep into the sugarcane fields they went,
through country roads, meadows, and lawns.

Arun and his parents bounced around,
while marveling at the beautiful sights.
It was an even more special day,
because it was Chikoo's first tractor ride.

Chikoo barked in sheer excitement,
when they passed some cows along the way.
They saw horses, other dogs, and even pigs,
"This is such a great start to the day!"

Little Arun cried out in delight,
when in the distance he could now see:
something majestic, so full of colours,
it was a peacock in a tree!

Arun sprang up from his seat,
he had never seen a peacock in his life.
With a vibrant, blue body, and emerald tail,
it was such a breathtaking sight!

After a few relaxed round of the fields,
to the resort, they ventured back.
Because Arun's mom wanted a cup of tea,
and all were now hungry for a snack.

They walked up to the resort,
and were greeted with a smile at the door.
Fresh sugarcane juice was offered,
and their appetites began to soar.

They were taken to their room in the garden,
which held a pleasant surprise.
It was covered in yellow balloons,
and blue streamers were hung on all sides.

On the bed, *"Congratulations"* was written,
and on the table sat cookies and a cake.
There was also a letter from the owner
that said: *"Arun, just for you,
these were all freshly baked!"*

After enjoying a delicious slice of cake,
and once his mom was done with her tea,
Arun and Chikoo went outside
to enjoy the fountains, flowers, and trees.

Arun's Weekend Getaway - Part 2

Chikoo ran freely in the grass,
enjoying all the smells and sounds.
And because this area was securely gated,
Chikoo was able to do countless rounds.

Arun's mom called him over,
telling him to come back in.
She asked him to change into his swimsuit,
so they could go for a little swim.

Arun changed into his costume,
and his family ventured towards the pool.
They reached it after following the cycling path,
and placed their towels on a stool.

Arun put on his gray goggles
and with confidence, jumped in.
His mom dipped her toes into the water,
while enjoying the sun on her skin.

After a few hours of fun and swimming,
on the horizon, the sun was starting to set.
The sky was streaked with various
shades of orange and pink,
it was a sight they would never forget.

Arun was now tired,
and his dad wanted to go to the room.
But his mom wanted to stay longer,
enjoying that her toes were starting to prune.

When back in the room, the boys first relaxed,
and then changed into their dry clothes.
With excitement, they went up to the terrace,
eager to try out the telescope.

"What a big telescope!" Arun said to his dad,
"The stars here shine so bright!"
Arun's dad replied:
*"Yes, and because the sky is so clear,
you can really enjoy the night!"*

The telescope was adjusted for Arun,
giving him a perfect view to see:
the glowing moon, the stars and constellations,
even Saturn's rings floating freely.

Arun's mom came up to the terrace,
and found the boys captivated by the sights.
Arun looked at his mom
with eyes filled with wonder,
which brought her immense delight.

"Come and look, Mom, at the stars,
I've never seen them ever so clear!"
His mom peeked into the telescope, and said:
"Amazing! We must come here every year!"

My Shadow

My shadow follows me around,
everywhere I go.
And every time I try to catch it,
I'm always too slow.
So I made a plan to trap it,
during the night before I sleep.
But when I turned off the light,
my shadow ran away from me.

Flying

I had a dream that I had wings,
and I was able to fly.
It was exciting until I learned that
I am afraid of heights!

Still, I kept on going higher,
I was unsure of how to land.
The wind stung at my eyes,
and things were getting out of hand.

Suddenly, I woke up,
and I was glad to see:
that instead of wings
I had my arms,
resting on the sides of me.

And that is when I realized,
it is better to walk on the ground;
than to soar and be afraid of the sky,
from which I cannot get down.

Hide and Cheese

It was an uneventful afternoon,
so Arun proposed a game of hide and seek.
He asked his mom to count down from thirty,
and made her promise not to peek.

He dashed out of the room,
and began to search around.
He carefully walked on his tiptoes,
making sure not to make a sound.

He searched throughout the house,
trying to find the perfect place to hide.
He looked under the beds
and opened up the closets,
wondering if he could squeeze inside.

But Arun was too big to fit in the closets,
which were filled with towels and clothes.
And if he hid behind the curtains,
she would surely spot his toes.

Time was running out…
soon his mom would be there.
But then an idea came to Arun:
to hide beneath the stairs!

He had just enough time to quickly crawl under,
and tuck himself in the back.
That is when he heard his mom above him
on the stairs, now starting to crack.

"Ready or not, here I come!"
echoed his mom's powerful yell.
And in that moment, he noticed
there was a rather unpleasant smell.

Arun quietly tried to look around,
but it was too dark for him to see.
Little did he know that he was sitting
next to a chunk of day-old cheese!

He desperately tried to cover his nose,
but nothing could reduce that horrid smell.
It took all of his strength not to cry out,
because he really wanted to yell.

His mom continued to look around,
while Arun hid beside the cheese.
He inhaled from his mouth,
and kept his nose shut by
continuing to hold and squeeze.

After five long, torturous minutes,
Arun could no longer continue to hide.
He rushed out from beneath the stairs,
hoping his mom was not close by.

But she was there, standing in front of him,
with a confused look on her face.
"I did not find you yet;
why'd you leave your hiding place?"

"Mom, it smells so bad under there!
Can you please go and check why?"
She bent down to look
with the light from her phone,
and saw cheese covered in small bites.

"Oh my god, no!" she cried out to Arun,
"What if we have a mouse?
That would be so bad; this is a huge problem,
we must check the entire house!"

Arun's mom suddenly turned towards Chikoo,
and that's when Arun finally saw:
it was his dog who was covered in cheese,
spread across his face, fur and paws!

When Chikoo saw them looking at him,
he jumped forward and grabbed the cheese.
Before they could stop him, he gobbled it up,
swallowing it down with ease.

Arun looked at his mom,
from her face the worry had washed away.
While laughing, she said to Arun,
"Looks like it's Chikoo's lucky day!"

They checked once more to ensure that
there was definitely no more cheese.
"Since I lost that time…"
Arun looked at his mom and requested:
"Can we have one more round, please?"

His mom went into the other room,
and started to count down once more.
But this time, Arun double-checked that
nothing smelly was left by Chikoo on the floor.

Missing Socks

Before Arun went to sleep,
he kept his socks on his bed.
But the next morning all that
remained was a single thread.

His socks were missing…
had they run away in the night?
He searched around for them,
but they were nowhere in sight.

He checked the washing machine,
and the hamper for dirty clothes.
His socks would have been safe,
if he'd just kept them on his toes.

He checked in every room,
and looked under every chair.
Then suddenly, he remembered:
Chikoo hides things under the stairs!

Arun crawled beneath the stairs,
and at last, he found:
both of his socks lying there,
in a pile on the ground.

Arun has become clever,
he's learned from days before.
Before bed, he now keeps his socks
safe inside his drawer.

Cycling through Delhi

Saturday mornings are when Arun
goes out with his dad to explore:
to see new things, to go new places,
and to learn about things more.

Like, why do the monkeys sit in trees?
And what is special about bumblebees?
Why do the cows stop on the road?
And why don't the street dogs do as they're told?

Arun put on his helmet,
and off the two boys went.
Happy to be out exploring,
knowing it will be a day well spent.

From a distance, Arun first saw
a family of monkeys in a tree.
"Are they not scared?
Why are they up there?"
He asked his dad, instantly.

His dad said: *"Do you know,*
my little Arun, why they sit so high?
It's so that they can protect themselves,
by keeping a lookout from the sky."

The boys then happily pedalled along,
enjoying the crisp morning breeze.
When from out of nowhere,
flying towards little Arun,
came two giant bumblebees!

"Dad! Dad! I need your help!"
Little Arun cried out, in fright.
His dad turned back, saw the bees,
and said, *"Arun, you will be alright!"*

"Bumblebees are usually nice,
and they very rarely sting...
they are out finding nectar for their hive,
for which they must collect and bring."

Arun wiped away his tears,
and gave his dad a hopeful smile.
He then replied:
"I haven't felt scared like this in a while!"

They continued to explore,
but found their path blocked by a big, hairy cow.
"Why is he here?" Little Arun protested,
"Tell him to move right now!"

His dad calmly responded:
"Arun, this road is open and free to use for all.
Including the animals who walk across,
no matter how big or small."

"We are all going someplace different,
and we must always understand:
that one journey is not more important
than another, this is everybody's land."

Arun's dad got off his bike,
and guided the cow to the park.
And once the cow was safe and secure,
on their journey they could now reembark.

And so, once more,
Arun and his dad got moving,
and they both continued to bike.
When a pack of dogs came out from the bushes,
looking angry and ready for a fight.

Arun yelled: *"Oh no!*
Dad, now what will we do?
I do not want to be bitten by the dogs,
I do not want to be dog food!"

Reassuringly, his dad replied:
"These dogs are harmless; they will not bite.
More than you, they are afraid -
can't you see they are filled with fright?"

"All living creatures are generally nice,
including that big cow down the road,
the bumblebees that we met before,
and the monkeys, both young and old."

"These outdoor dogs are also not dangerous,
and I assure you, they will not attack.
Just show them kindness and respect,
and they'll return the same thing back."

After Arun's dad gave his speech,
the dogs started to wag their tails.
And they gave way for Arun and his dad,
to continue on their trail.

The boys finally returned home,
after spending the day outdoors.
Though Arun felt a bit tired,
he'd never had so much fun before.

That night, as he got ready for bed,
Arun was still feeling excited.
So he told his mom, *"For my birthday,*
please make sure all the animals are invited!"

Arun's Birthday Bash

"Today is the day!"
Little Arun was excited to say:
*"For my birthday, all my friends will come,
and so many games we will play!"*

*"Today is the day!
I cannot believe that it has arrived so soon!*
Arun exclaimed: *"School is over,
the weather is hot, how is it already June?"*

Today is the day!
Arun's mom was setting up the decor.
There were orange balloons on the walls,
blue hats on the table,
and green streamers hanging on the door.

Today is the day!
Arun's dad was taking out the cake -
with icing a big blue sky was drawn,
along with mountains and a lake.

Today's the day!
Arun eagerly waited for his friends by the door.
One by one, he imagined they would walk in,
greeting Chikoo on the floor.

Today's the day!
It is already 2:00 PM…and no one has arrived.
Did he make a mistake on the invitation?
Did his mom forget to remind?

"Today's the day!"
Little Arun continued to say,
with less excitement and a frown.
"Why has no one come to see me?
I am feeling so let down."

"Today's the day?"
Arun felt the need to cross-check with his dad.
And with a giggle, his father said:
"Little Arun, please do not be sad…"

"Because today is the day that you were born,
and we do have a lot in store.
But you must stop counting down the minutes,
and staring at the door!"

"But, how can I not?"
Little Arun looked away, as he softly replied -
with a swollen face, and with crossed arms,
he had tears in his eyes.

His mom gently grabbed Arun's hand,
and slowly walked him outside to the park.
Where Arun saw all his friends
waiting there for him,
and in excitement, Chikoo started to bark!

There was Esha, Priya, Pooja,
Ranveer, Rajveer, and even Dhruv!
"You were all here waiting for me?
This is a dream come true!"

And to add to the joy, all the friendly animals,
that he met biking with his dad:
crossed through the park to see him,
to make sure that he was glad.

Arun and his friends started to play games,
and they were now having a lot of fun.
And with a smile, Arun could finally say:
"Today's the day! It's my birthday!
Thanks for coming, everyone!"

A Race to Remember

I proposed a race to my friend,
because I was sure that I would win.
When suddenly, he took off running,
before I could even begin.

I tried my best to catch up with him,
but he was too far ahead.
My legs started to feel like jelly,
and my face was turning bright red.

Suddenly, I remembered,
that I had a trick up my sleeve!
My secret shortcut, through the trees and bushes,
that no one would ever believe.

And so, I ran off the road,
and into the woods so deep.
I leaped over the vines
and avoided all the branches,
making sure not to lose any speed.

I jumped out from the forest,
and back onto the main path again.
I looked ahead in front of me,
but I could not spot my friend.

I then heard my name from behind me…
which is why I turned around -
only to watch him pass me a second time,
with his feet barely touching the ground.

He was close to the finish line,
when he turned back with a grin.
"*Nice try,*" he said while laughing,
as he sprinted ahead to win.

I laughed too, though defeated,
because it was all in good fun.
For it's not just about winning,
but the joy of the chase and the run.

A Creepy Crawly Encounter

It was a pleasant night until Arun spotted:
a sneaky spider on his wall.
With its chunky body and eight hairy legs,
the little critter began to crawl.

Up and down the wall it went,
and across from left to right.
It was moving all over the room,
filling Arun with immense fright.

"I can see its legs!" screamed little Arun,
who was completely frozen with fear.
"What if it lays thousands of eggs?
What if it decides to stay here?"

*"I think I can handle one spider -
at the most, maybe two or three...
But I am definitely not okay sharing
my room with an entire colony!"*

Arun watched carefully,
the thin web it started to spin.
*"Yuck, how is it doing that?
How does it have a thread within?"*

After hearing all the commotion,
Arun's dad came in and sat by his side.
"Spiders produce their own silk thread,"
he explained,
"to weave a web where they can hide."

*"Though they seem a bit creepy,
that much even I can agree.
This spider is simple looking for a place,
where it can live danger-free."*

*"But let us do one thing,
together we'll find it a new home.
Somewhere safe in the outdoor,
so that in your room it will not roam."*

"But how will we catch it?"
Arun confidently pointed out:
"It is right above my bed!
What if it runs or jumps off the wall,
and then lands here on my head?"

Arun's dad got a clear bowl,
and gently contained the spider inside.
Slowly, he carried it up to the roof,
and released it, so that it could hide.

A little corner in the shade,
is where the spider spun a new web.
And the spider now had a home of its own,
far away from Arun's bed.

A Walk in the Park - Part 1

It has been a long summer,
and the weather has been hot.
The afternoon sky is again clear,
but Arun knows a shaded spot.

It is at the end of the park,
across all the areas for sports.
Through the places for cricket,
football and basketball,
as well as all the other courts.

Under the blaring sun,
Arun set out on his path…
from walking he began to run,
to get out of the sun's wrath.

He first crossed the cricket field,
where the kids lined up for batting;
the teenagers who should have caught the ball,
missed it because they were busy chatting.

Thankfully, Arun was able to cross
safely and with ease…
to reach the vast football field,
surrounded by bushes and leaves.

"*Messi is my favorite!*"
He heard one of the older boys say.
"*No way, it is Ronaldo who is the best!*
Haven't you ever watched him play?"

Arun did not watch sports,
so he did not know who was better.
But he liked the blue logo that said '*Chelsea,*'
that was visible on one boy's sweater.

From the football field,
Arun walked to reach the basketball court -
where he stopped to admire all the players,
because it is his favorite sport.

While avoiding the big orange ball,
Arun bolted to the other side.
The older kids did not notice,
because he was still small and not very wide.

Arun reached the end of the park,
filled with many kids who always played.
And there stood his favorite tree,
which always provided him with shade.

It was a magnificent Neem tree,
that stood almost 20 meters in height!
Even from the start of the park,
Arun could spot it from morning to night.

When Arun finally sat down,
and wiped the sweat off his face;
he could not help but smile,
because he was sitting in his favorite place.

A Walk in the Park - Part 2

Arun leisurely sat
under his favorite tree,
feeling calm without a fret.
When he suddenly realized that
soon it would be night,
because the sun was starting to set.

Arun knew he had to be back home
before it got dark.
That was the rule his mom had set,
before he went to the park.

And so, he jumped up from his seat,
and quickly began to jog.
He was excited to see his parents,
and also Chikoo, his furry dog.

He ran so fast, faster than he ever had,
because he was excited to reach his home.
Where his family was patiently waiting,
and Arun would no longer have to be alone.

In his mind, Arun was already planning
all the things that he wanted to say:
From watching the kids playing their sports,
to reaching his favourite seat in the shade.

Before even realizing it,
he was already back to square one.
Arun was at the start of the cricket field,
where his afternoon journey had begun.

At the top of the stairs,
he was greeted by his parents,
with their arms held open wide.
And together, they told little Arun:
"You must hug us before you come inside!"

He happily ran into their arms,
and they held him close and tight.
Proudly, Arun said to his mom:
"See, I told you I'd be home before night!"

His mom said, *"Of course,
Arun, that much I already knew.
For now, you are still young,
and you must stick to your curfew."*

"*But we are glad that you listened,
and that you came well on time -
because now we have the whole evening
to sit together and unwind.*"

Sunday Delight

Every Sunday,
Arun visits his nana and nani.
And for little Arun,
she always cooks a very special feast.

Arun never knows what his nani will cook,
because she loves to give him a surprise.
Last week she had made rajma-chawal,
served with fresh raita on the side.

During the long car ride,
Arun tried to imagine
what all his nani might have made…
It could be tikkis, aloo burgers,
some savory sandwiches,
maybe there was even fresh lemonade!

Once they reached, Arun's dad stopped
in search of a place to park outside.
Arun leaped out of the car, ran up to the door,
desperate to sneak a peek inside.

He could see that the table was set
with fresh flowers in the center.
But what was kept inside the casseroles,
he would only find out when he entered.

His nani came to open the door,
and Arun touched her feet.
He could then smell a minty aroma,
hinting at a tasty treat.

As soon as he could smell the chutney,
little Arun instantly knew…
there must be fresh parathas waiting,
even if they weren't in his view!

His nani took him to the table,
and asked him to look inside.
But when Arun opened up the casserole,
there were no parathas in sight.

It took Arun a moment to recognize
the white oval-shaped treat.
His nani had made idlis with sambar,
and they were ready for him to eat.

The smell that he thought was mint,
was actually coconut mixed with spice.
It was made with a lot of time and care,
to accompany the fluffy steamed rice.

She made Arun a big full plate,
when nana suddenly appeared.
He asked, *"Is that plate for me?"*
while grinning from ear to ear.

Arun's nana was only a few minutes late
because he had gone to the store -
to pick up some butter, and a packet of milk,
which he had kept in the refrigerator door.

Arun's nani had used up these items,
and she urgently needed them to bake -
something fresh and delicious for Arun:
a scrumptious strawberry cream cake!

While everyone was distracted by eating,
she sneaked away to make the batter.
She mixed in the flour, butter, eggs, and milk,
her hand was steady to avoid any splatter.

She placed the cake in the oven,
then sat back at the table to eat.
She paced her bites to the sound of the timer,
knowing that soon she would serve her treat.

She got up to take out the cake,
even before the timer made a sound.
In just a few minutes, the cake was garnished,
and she called everyone to gather around.

Arun was the first to indulge
in her delicious, sweet surprise.
And as everyone enjoyed the cake,
tears of joy filled her eyes.

Happily, she told her family,
"Today's lunch was made with a lot of care.
And I'm already planning next week's menu,
so save your appetites and come prepared."

With a big, full tummy,
Arun said goodbye to his nana and nani.
What will she have in store for next week?
He will just have to wait and see.

Nightmares

It was the crack of dawn,
and Arun couldn't ignore
the sound of birds chirping outside.
Through the gaps in his curtains,
the light slowly entered his room,
shining into his eyes.

Arun still wanted to get more sleep,
and did not want to get out of bed.
So he turned over to the other side,
and pulled the blanket over his head.

His mom peeked in,
and as the door opened
Arun could hear a soft creak.
He did not open his eyes,
nor did he move his body,
while he pretended to be fast asleep.

She walked up to the bed, sat by his side,
and gently gave him a little shake.
"My dearest Arun, why are you still lying down?
I have a feeling that you're awake..."

Arun pulled down the covers,
gazing up at his mom with a sad, timid face.
*"Last night I had so many bad dreams,
my mind was all over the place!"*

*"First, I dreamt that I was stuck outside,
and that the house door was locked.
I kept banging and begging to come inside,
but no one answered my knocks."*

*"Then, suddenly, I started shrinking,
I became the size of a flea...
and no matter how hard you look around,
because of my size: you could not find me!"*

His mom held Arun in a warm, soft hug,
gently cradling him in her arms.
*"My little one, there's nothing to fear;
I'll always keep you safe from harm."*

She said this to Arun,
with a kiss upon his head.
*"Sit up, I'm right here with you -
it's now time to get out of bed."*

*"We'll always leave the door open for you,
so there's no need for fright.
And even if you're as tiny as a flea,
I'll find you, day or night."*

"The next time that you have bad dreams,
remember that we are always near.
Come snuggle into our bed,
our love will overcome your fear."

"I also know what caused your scary dreams:
it was the sweets you had before bed.
Rather than your usual happy thoughts,
your mind was filled with worries instead."

"This evening we will not have sugar,
and I promise you will see:
you will sleep well, there'll be no bad dreams,
and tomorrow you'll wake up happily."

That night Arun went to sleep
without any late-night snacks.
And to his surprise, his mom was right,
the nightmares did not come back.

The Tooth - Part 1

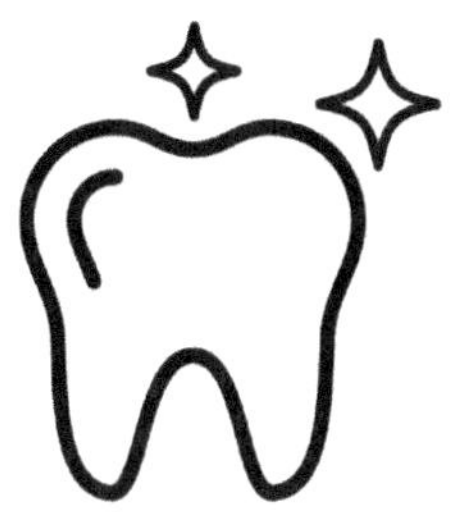

"I lost a tooth!"
Little Arun cried out,
for his parents to look
at the hole in his mouth.

"I lost a tooth,
it's here in my hand.
It fell out of my gums,
I do not understand..."

"...why it has fallen,
what should I do?
When I try to smile,
you can see right through!"

"How will I bite?
How can I eat?
How will I chew
with so few teeth?"

*"I lost two already,
now I'm missing three.
Why are these teeth
falling out of me?"*

*"Will I have no teeth left?
That's a horrible thought.
I took them for granted
when I had a lot."*

*"I thought they were strong,
I thought they would stay.
This tooth in my hand…
was in my mouth yesterday."*

*"What will I do now?
I surrender to defeat.
I refuse to smile
without all my teeth."*

The Tooth - Part 2

Arun's dad gently lifted the tooth
from his son's tiny palm.
With reassurance in his voice, he said,
"No need to worry, Arun, stay calm."

"This is only a baby tooth!
They must go so that there is space:
for your adult teeth to grow in,
and take their rightful place."

"One day you will also have big teeth,
just like your dad and mom!
And you'll have a big, beautiful smile,
that will last you all life long."

"But you are very lucky,
because now you get a wish -
from the Tooth Fairy,
who collects these teeth,
from all the young kids."

"For this special tooth of yours,
she'll give you a wonderful surprise!
Just remember to place it
under your pillow tonight,
right before you close your eyes."

And so, that night,
Arun kept the tooth,
just as his father had said.
And when he woke up, he spotted a box,
carefully placed right next to his bed.

Arun opened it up, expecting a gift,
but all he found was a note.
On the paper, written in green ink,
the Tooth Fairy had wrote:

"For your kindness,
I will grant you one wish.
Would you like a new toy?
Just write it on the back of this letter.
Thank you for the tooth, sweet little boy!"

Arun grinned with delight,
and his mind began to race.
What should he wish for?
His thoughts flew all over the place.

He pondered a shiny bike,
or perhaps a talking bear.
Maybe a trip to the zoo,
or a kite to fly in the air.

But then, suddenly, he paused,
and instantly Arun knew.
He did not need a new toy,
Arun needed a new tooth!

With a red crayon he scribbled
these words on the letter's backside:
*"Dear Tooth Fairy, please fill the
holes in my mouth that are so wide."*

*"It feels so strange to me…
with many of my teeth gone.
Can you fill the gaps with some teeth,
that are healthy and strong?"*

*"Not just for me,
but for all of my friends, too.
I wish for our grown-up teeth
to come in shiny and new."*

Afterwards, Arun felt relieved,
and he no longer had any fear.
Because he now knew that the Tooth Fairy
would make all his new teeth appear.

Feeling the Blues over Ripped Shoes

It was a regular morning,
when Arun went to put on his blue shoes.
He soon realized that through the tops,
his toes were poking through.

They were now too small for him,
when did his feet grow in size?
Arun had already grown in height,
but this was an unwanted surprise.

He didn't know that other parts of his body
would also stretch and grow.
And now, in addition to his height and hair,
there were clear changes in his toes.

When he looked in the mirror,
it was obvious that he was growing.
He already noticed that he felt bigger,
but now it was also showing!

Was his nose always this pointy?
And were his eyebrows always so thick?
"Mom!" Arun yelled, *"Please come inside,"*
I think I'm going to be sick!"

"What is going on with me?
Somehow my shoe tops are torn.
There's a weird beauty mark on my arm,
was it here when I was born?"

"My pants are also feeling tight,
and they are too short in length.
Everyone can see my socks,
I do not have the strength…"

"…To process all of these changes,
today I cannot go to school.
If I show up looking like this,
everyone will think that I'm not cool!"

His mom started to giggle,
and told Arun, *"You can stay home today.*
You have no classes because school is closed,
did you forget it's Saturday?"

"How about we go to the mall,
and buy you some new clothes?
Pants that fit you just right,
and shoes that cover your toes."

"As for the rest of the changes,
it is normal that it feels a bit weird.
Just wait until you're a teenager,
and you start growing a beard!"

"It is all completely normal,
your body will continue to grow;
but nothing happens overnight,
and the changes will come out slow."

"So don't worry about looking odd,
because your friends are changing, too!
Embrace your new appearance,
because although it's a bit different,
you'll always be you."

Be careful with Swings

When you get on a swing,
you can swing so high,
you can swing your
way up to the sky.

You can swing in the clouds.
You can swing over the trees.
You can soar in the sky,
like the birds and the bees.

You can see over the houses,
you can see over the town.
How different the world appears,
when you look from up to down.

But you need to be careful
because if you swing too high,
you can accidentally end up
soaring over our sky!

And you'll go straight into space,
next to the big planets that float.
Where it is freezing cold,
without an astronaut's coat.

So although it is tempting,
do not gain too much height;
Or we might see you floating,
next to the yellow moon tonight.

A Letter from Abroad

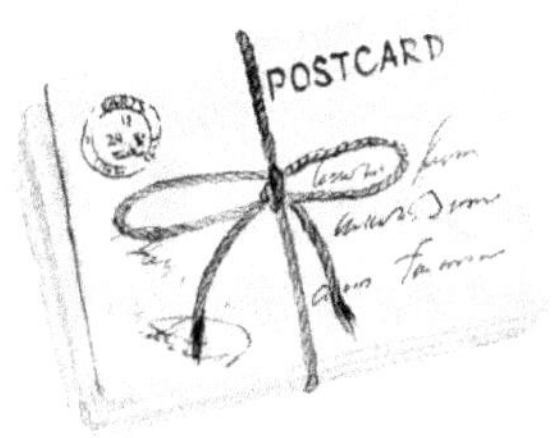

"Hey there, Mr. Postman!
What's that in your hand?
Is there a letter for me,
from my cousin in a far-off land?"

"Hey there, Mr. Postman!
Please have a look and see:
if in your bag, there is a letter,
that is addressed to me?"

"Or it could be for my dad...
maybe it's marked to my mom?
Last week I sent out an important letter,
and it took me very long..."

"...to find the words that I wanted to say
to my cousin who lives abroad.
I told him about all my recent journeys,
even the ones I took with my dog!"

"I told him that I would love to see him,
and that I hope he visits soon.
He could come now and enjoy the rain,
because it is almost time for the monsoon."

"He can play with Chikoo,
and come for Sunday lunch with me.
I'm sure that he would love to taste
the food made by my nani."

"Dear Mr. Postman,
I am still waiting for your update.
Has his response arrived?
Or will I still have to wait?"

In his bag, the postman looked,
and he found an envelope.
It was addressed to Arun, stamped from Canada,
and it was wrapped in a red rope.

The contents of the letter read:
"Dearest Arun, your letters are so fun.
Thank you for writing to me,
I cherish every one!"

"I have good news!
My mom told me we'll be visiting you soon.
But I don't know the exact date;
I hope to see the monsoon."

*"It is summer here in Canada,
soon it will be autumn.
You should come and see the colorful leaves
which fall from treetop to bottom."*

*"I'd much rather be there with you,
I will call you when I know:
the date of our flight -
I'm really looking forward
to all the places we'll go!"*

Full of excitement, Arun ran to show his mom
the kind handwritten letter.
She then replied to Arun, *"Yes, they
are making their travel arrangements.
Could anything be better?"*

*"But for now, we have to patiently wait,
to find out when they will come.
But there's one thing that I know for sure:
when they arrive we will have lots of fun!"*

Ding Dong!

It was 6:45 in the morning,
when there was a knock on the front door.
What an unusual time for someone to arrive,
it must be a person he'd never met before.

The doorbell now rang.
Who could it be…so early in the day?
Arun stayed in his bed,
assuming the person would eventually go away.

Ding dong!
The doorbell rang again,
shaking the entire house.
He could feel the vibrations of the bell
moving in his body, throughout.

Why hadn't anyone gotten up yet,
to open the door and see?
Who was waiting at the gate,
and that too, so impatiently!

Ding dong!
Someone rang again,
Arun finally jumped out of his bed.
"Who would ring the bell three times?"
Arun thought, while scratching his head.

When Arun walked out of his room,
his parents were waiting there for him.
With frustration, he asked,
"If there's someone waiting outside…
why were they not let in?"

His mom, with a giggle, told Arun:
"You are the one who must open the gate.
The guest has already rung the bell three times,
for how long will they wait?"

Arun was very confused,
when he walked up to the front door.
And to his surprise, waiting there
was his cousin from Canada whom he adored!

"Luca? Is that really you?"
Exclaimed Arun, with a smile.
"Did you not hear me? Luca asked,
I've been ringing the bell for quite a while!"

Arun quickly unlocked the door,
and gave his cousin a heartfelt hug.
Then came Chikoo, who jumped on Luca,
giving his shirt a playful tug.

While trying to pick up Chikoo,
who was rolling all over the floor -
from behind came Luca's parents,
now waiting at the door.

*"Mami, Mama! You're also here?
What a pleasant treat!"*
Arun rushed over to greet them,
and took blessings by touching their feet.

*"Please everyone, do come inside,
I can't believe that you're all finally here.
I have been eagerly waiting for your arrival,
I thought about it every day this year!"*

In sheer excitement, Arun asked:
"Where will you all stay?"
His aunt replied,
"Here with you, if that is okay?"

Arun's face lit up as he said,
"Of course, this is such amazing news!
Luca can sleep with me, I have an extra pillow,
and I'll set the bed for two."

"I cannot wait to take Luca around,
there are so many games we can play.
I have so many places for us to explore,
what an amazing start to the day!"

"Next time that the doorbell rings,
I will not wait so long.
I never thought it would be for me,
how could I have been so wrong?"

"I still cannot believe it,
together we will have so much fun..."
And to that, Luca replied to Arun:
"Yes, our holiday together has finally begun!"

The Boys explore

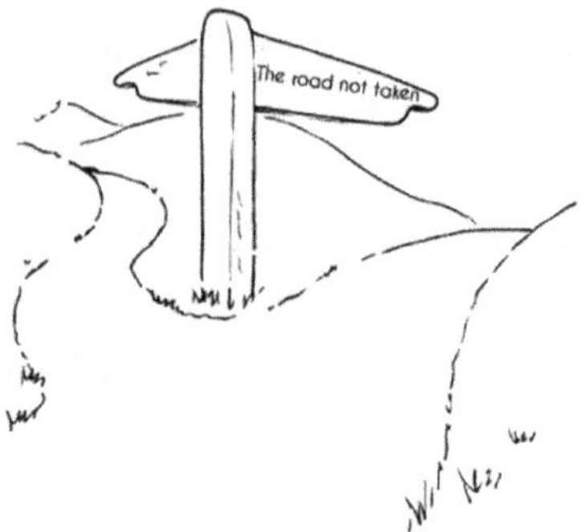

Arun was determined to show his cousin
all the best places in his hometown.
They rode their bikes together,
exploring the neighborhood -
pedalling all the way around.

Arun took Luca to his secret spot,
to sit in his favourite shaded seat.
He also took Luca to the other park,
where his nana planted the mango tree.

Arun took Luca to the same bike path,
where he and his dad had explored -
Hoping to show him the animals there,
the ones he so deeply adored.

Arun's family took Luca to see India Gate,
and the towering Qutub Minar!
They also enjoyed a scenic country drive,
on their way to Namaste Dwaar.

Another thing which was exciting,
is that they got to see new sights.
They drove all the way to Agra,
to see the Taj Mahal in all its might.

Arun and Luca liked all the same things,
both were sad the trip would end.
And the best part of their adventure,
was when they realized they were
not just cousins, they were now best friends.

Which meant that even though they both lived,
thousands of miles apart.
The two boys would always be connected,
through mind and through the heart.

Puddles of Rain

The clock struck two, and out of the blue,
it started to rain outside.
When Arun heard the sound of rain,
only one thought crossed his mind.

Arun rushed to find his rubber boots,
he was desperate to venture out.
His plan was simple:
to find the biggest puddle he could
to jump in and stomp around.

He put on Chikoo's leash,
and the boys were ready to step outside.
He adjusted his hood, pulled up his pants,
and double checked that Chikoo was tied.

Arun said goodbye to his parents,
and the boys dashed out the door.
Chikoo could now smell the muddy ground,
waiting to be explored.

The boys reached the street,
finally feeling the rain from up in the skies.
And the raindrops which slid off Arun's coat,
dripped down right into Chikoo's eyes.

Chikoo shook off the excess water,
so that he could look ahead and see.
And that's when Chikoo took off running,
pulling Arun across the street.

They almost collided with a tree,
but thankfully Chikoo abruptly stopped.
He looked up at Arun,
who was still catching his breath,
and into a puddle, Chikoo hopped!

When Arun looked down,
Chikoo was wagging his tail,
and beneath him…Arun finally saw:
It was Chikoo who found
the biggest puddle of rain,
and Arun was left in awe.

Chikoo barked at Arun,
urging him to also jump inside.
Arun smiled and said,
"Okay! One, two, three!"
Then he leaped forward,
with a grin so wide.

The water splashed everywhere
when Arun's feet finally hit the ground.
Chikoo jumped out of the way,
startled by the sudden, thunderous sound.

For hour and hours,
Arun and Chikoo joyfully explored.
They ran around, played in puddles,
and fully enjoyed the rain as it poured.

Arun loved being in the rain,
and he loved having Chikoo by his side.
But if they didn't head back soon,
he knew his boots would never be dried.

Once back home, Arun said to his mom,
"I wish the rain would never go away!"
His mom replied, *"Arun, it's special
because it does not happen every day."*

*"You appreciate the rain after too much sun,
and you'll miss the sun if it goes to hide.
Enjoy the magic in every situation—
the grass isn't always greener on the other side."*

Arun thought for a while, then said:
*"You're right, Mom, it is true.
I really do love the rain,
but I also love the sun, too."*

*"Each brings its own joy,
in its own perfect way.
And with both in my life,
I wouldn't want it any other way."*

Arun's Alphabet Song

Arun's teacher asked him,
to compose a fun new song.
So that he could learn his letters,
and never get them wrong.

This is what Arun wrote,
so that he would not forget…
what letters come between
'A to Z,' in the alphabet:

A is for ALL the times
that I go outside to play.
B is for the BUMBLEBEES,
that fly along the way.

C if for the CLOUDS,
which protect me from the sun.
D is for DREAMS
where my imagination runs!

E is for EVERY time that
my mom makes me laugh.
F is for all the FUN I have
riding bikes with my Dad.

G is for GOING out with
my friends and family.
H is for HOLIDAYS,
which make me feel so free.

I is for IMAGINATION,
which makes everything more fun.
J is for all the new JOURNEYS
that have not yet begun.

K is for KEEPING spiders
outside of my room.
L is for LONGING to feel
the rain from the monsoon.

M is for the MONKEYS,
that sit high upon the trees.
N is for all the NEW places
that I have yet to see.

O if for OFFICE,
where my dad goes every day.
P is for PLEASE let me
go outside and play!

Q is for QUIET time,
when I like to sit and read.
R is for RACING,
especially when I am in the lead!

S is for SCHOOL,
where I love to go and learn.
T is for managing my TIME,
which is always a concern.

U is for UNDERSTANDING
that sometimes things go wrong.
V is for it's VERY fun to
sing and dance to songs.

W is for wondering WHERE
I will go next to explore?
X is for needing X-RAYS if
I fall too hard on the floor.

Y is for YOU have the power to
become whoever you want to be.
Z is for 3,2,1 ZERO,
when I countdown from three!

It is always easier to learn things,
when you make them into a song.
The melody helps the memory,
and the rhythm keeps it strong.

From the alphabet to numbers,
and the planets in the sky,
next time you want to learn something new:
give this simple trick a try.

Brushing your Teeth before Bed

Once Arun finished his homework,
his mom said, "Time to brush your teeth."
He asked, "Which ones do I need to brush?"
She joked, "Only the ones you want to keep!"

"Mom, I want to keep them all!"
Replied Arun, with concern on his face.
*"From now on, I'll scrub each and every
tooth at least twice, just in case!"*

Arun went to the bathroom,
and squeezed some paste onto his brush.
To clean each tooth properly,
he took his time and didn't rush.

He then proceeded to floss his teeth,
making sure nothing was caught in between.
He rinsed out the paste, then dried his face,
his mouth felt fresh and clean.

When Arun's mom came to check on him,
she reminded him of one thing left to do:
Now that his teeth were clean and bright,
she wanted to wash his hair with shampoo.

Once Arun was done bathing,
he then put on some fresh clothes.
And that night, he had the best sleep ever,
feeling clean from his head to his toes.

The next morning, after a restful night,
Arun made a vow to remember:
if you brush your teeth and bathe every night,
you will always sleep better!

Spilled Milk

Unfortunately, at times,
things will not go as you've planned.
Arun had to learn this the hard way,
when one morning got out of hand.

Arun was trying, so very hard,
to be his absolute best.
He got good grades, he slept on time,
but his mind was never at rest.

That day, he woke up extra early
to take his time getting ready for school.
But when he spilled milk on his sweater,
Arun suddenly lost his cool.

Arun was upset and began to cry,
his mom found him on the floor.
With concern, she asked, *"What is wrong?
What are you crying for?"*

*"I spilled some milk on my new sweater,
and now it is covered in tears."*
Arun replied, glancing away from his mom,
feeling a mix of worry and fear.

"Is that all that happened?
My precious Arun, please do not be sad.
It was only an accident, you spilled some milk,
how could I ever be mad?"

"You're being too hard on yourself,
by holding your standards so high.
It's important to be patient with yourself,
and when you're sad, to let yourself cry."

"No one expects you to be perfect,
we all fall short sometimes.
We all make messes, we all make mistakes.
Don't beat yourself up, you're doing just fine!"

"The important thing to remember:
is that nothing is as bad as it may seem.
Take a deep breath, and try to relax,
we are always on your team."

"Now, Arun, hand me your glass...
I'll show you that everything's okay."
His mom took a sip of the milk,
only to let it drip all over her face.

The milk went down her chin,
and collected on her shirt.
It formed a puddle on the floor,
and left marks across her skirt!

Arun kept staring at his mom,
he was completely shocked.
She was standing in a puddle of milk,
it had seeped into her socks.

The sight was so ridiculous,
Arun could not help but laugh.
"Mom, what's going on?
I need to take a photograph!"

She replied, *"Seeing your bright smile*
is truly my favourite sight.
And you should never cry over spilled milk;
let nothing in life fill you with fright."

"Now let's go change,
and then we can eat some tasty food.
There's nothing better than a warm breakfast,
to put you in a good mood."

Together they sat at the table, giggling,
about the dramatic start to the day.
Then Arun turned to his mom, and said,
"You're right, it wasn't a big deal anyway."

Bye for Now…

Hello everyone,
this is Arun writing,
I hope that you enjoyed my tales.
Thank you all for sticking with me,
I bid each one of you farewell!

So long, everyone!
It is now time to say goodbye:
to all my new friends,
who have journeyed with me,
to new places far and wide.

I hope that you have a great day today,
and an even greater year.
I'll keep writing out my adventures,
so there's always something new to hear.

I hope to meet you all one day,
I'm so happy to have new friends.

But for now, I am off exploring new places, so that our journey together never ends.

Sincerely,

Your newest and truest friend…*Arun!*

www.ingramcontent.com/pod-product-compliance
Lightning Source LLC
LaVergne TN
LVHW020346200726
843507LV00012B/2516